MOTHER TERESA

LIVING IN LOVE

MOTHER TERESA

LIVING IN LOVE

A Compilation of Mother Teresa's
Teachings on Love

GLENNA HAMMER MOULTHROP

TowleHouse Publishing Company, Inc.
Nashville, Tennessee

An extensive effort has been made to identify the many sources of Mother Teresa's quotations in this collection. In addition to those listed in the bibliography, these sources include TV specials, speeches, church bulletins, and random notes the author has kept over the past fifteen years. If there are any omissions or oversights, we apologize and will make suitable acknowledgments in future printings.

Library of Congress Cataloging-in-Publication Data

Teresa, Mother, 1910-
   Living in love : a compilation of Mother Teresa's teachings on love / Mother Teresa ; [compiled by] Glenna Hammer Moulthrop.
      p. cm.
   Includes bibliographical references (p. 107)
   ISBN 0-9668774-1-1
   1. Love--Religious aspects--Catholic Church. I. Moulthrop, Glenna Hammer, 1948- II. Title.
BV4639.T44 2000
241'.4--dc21
99-088406

Page design by Ed Curtis

Printed in the United States of America

1 2 3 4 5 6—04 03 02 01 00

*To my teacher, whose loving spirit grows in me
and speaks to me, especially in the silences*

CONTENTS

ILLUSTRATIONS

"God writes through us, and however imperfect instruments we may be, He writes beautifully."

—Mother Teresa

ACKNOWLEDGMENTS

God not only writes through us, He provides whatever we need to accomplish His work. I'd like to thank the Great Mysterious One for giving me the opportunity and means to do this book, particularly just the right people to guide and help me in many loving ways. I'm very grateful for:

Mama and Papa, Genie and Glen Hammer, who were the first ones to teach me how good it feels to be loved and to love and do for others;

my beautiful daughters Sarah and Emily, who offer me new lessons in love, joy, patience, and humility every day;

loving sisters Cindie Beaty and Marilyn Strankman, and wonderful nephews, Donald, Zachary, and Elliott, who are my heart's delight;

former bosses Jim Gallagher and LaMar Trego, who eased me gently into a new life, one that took me into Washington, D.C., and led me to "Gift of Peace," the Missionaries of Charity's hospice there;

colleague Jonathon Finley, for finding "Gift of Peace";

Sister Pietra, who opened her heart and "Gift of Peace" to me, and then held me in her prayers;

dear friend and "research assistant" Dotty Nolan, who shares my deep admiration for Mother Teresa, and always gives me new articles and books about her, as do Becky Rupp and Ghislaine Guignon;

capable friends-turned-literary-assistants Kathy Kilbury, Laurie Beitel, Bill Jacobi, Ron Hart, and the Rev. Dr. Jim Dyson, who each reviewed the first draft and provided excellent comments;

many other caring friends, especially Steve Muller, who often asked about this project and offered new ideas and encouraging words—usually when they were needed most;

and finally, Mike Towle of TowleHouse Publishing, for believing that we all need more of Mother Teresa's wisdom just as we need more of her kind of love.

MISSIONARIES of CHARITY

+L.D.M.

54 A, A.J.C. BOSE ROAD
CALCUTTA 700016 INDIA

Dear Glenna Moulthrop,

Thank you for your letter. This
brings you my prayers for God's
blessings on all that you do, and,
also on your book 'Living in Love'.
Do all for the glory of God

Keep the joy of loving God ever
burning in your heart.
Let us pray.

GOD BLESS YOU.

la Teresa mc

THE PALM LEAF

As Christ entered Jersusalem days before His crucifixion, He was honored by those who threw palms onto His path. Since that day—nearly two thousand years ago—the palm leaf has been a Christian symbol of triumph.

The life of Mother Teresa, matriarch of the Missionaries of Charity, who serve the poor and dying throughout the world, also symbolizes such a triumph. Her message, like Christ's, is eternal: only love—pure, unconditional, self-sacrificing love—triumphs over all things.

*"My vocation is love . . . I will <u>be</u> love
and then I will be all things."*

—*Saint Thérèse of Lisieux*

MOTHER TERESA
BIOGRAPHY

When Agnes Gonxha Bojaxhiu took her vows with the Order of Loreto in 1928, she took the name "Teresa" for her religious life. In doing so she made a sacred pact to follow her patron saint, Saint Thérèse of Lisieux, whose vocation was love. Indeed, Mother Teresa lived a life of love.

At age twelve, young Agnes already knew she wanted to be a missionary and serve others. At eighteen, she joined the Institute of the Blessed Virgin Mary (Loreto Sisters), an order known for its missionary work in India. Sister Teresa, as she was known then, trained first in Dublin and later in Darjeeling, India.

During her first eighteen years in India, Sister Teresa fulfilled her calling as a teacher and then as principal of Saint Mary's High School in Calcutta. In 1946, however, she received her "call within a call" and was divinely ordered to do God's work among the destitute and dying on the streets. Teresa was, in fact, called to living that same life of poverty.

Two years later, in 1948, she was given formal permission by the church to leave the Loreto Sisters and begin a new order. And within months, Teresa's mission of love began in the slums of Calcutta. That same year, she started her first school. By 1950, Mother Teresa had founded the Missionaries of Charity, and two years later she opened a home for the dying in Calcutta.

For nearly fifty years Mother Teresa devoted her life to serving God by serving those in great need—the unwanted ones, the abandoned, the dying, and the destitute. From such a simple beginning of one school for poor children in 1948, Mother Teresa and her Missionaries of Charity, buoyed by their faith and endless compassion, have brought hope to the needy in 120 countries.

Today, more than two years after Mother Teresa's death, her mission of love—unconditional and self-sacrificing love—continues in more than six hundred homes and centers worldwide.

INTRODUCTION

I've always been fascinated by powerful quotations. In their brevity, there's much wisdom. And there's plenty of room for one to think about how a quotation fits with her experiences. For me, quotations are great teachers. Their power is in their simplicity.

The same is true of Mother Teresa, whose life I've studied for years. Her power came from simplicity, too—a simple life grounded in God and shored up by faith and love. Since I've long been an admirer of Mother Teresa, and of a good quotation, it was natural for me to want to blend these two compelling interests in a collection of her teachings on love. All I had to do was follow Mother's lead.

Four years ago I traded a title in the corporate world for a more simple life. When concerned friends asked me why, I told them that I wanted to "live in love." Little did I know how much I had to learn. My own story, of difficult and painful lessons, is interwoven with Mother Teresa's teachings because writing this book was my primer. Through this experience, I feel like I've passed

21

kindergarten. I now know with certainty that, for most of us, living and growing in love will be a lifelong lesson. I hope this book helps you as you learn, too.

—Glenna Hammer Moulthrop

MOTHER TERESA

LIVING IN
LOVE

In a word, there are three things that
last forever: faith, hope, and love,
but the greatest of these is love.

—1 Corinthians 13:13

"Where there is mystery, there must be faith. Faith, you cannot change no matter how you look at it."

—Mother Teresa

I

THE INNER VOICE

In recent years my faith has deepened as I have come to see more clearly how God reveals Himself and His purpose for our lives in strange and mysterious ways. There are no coincidences in this life—only signs from God that we are on the right path. These signs come as feelings, welling up from deep within us. If we open our hearts completely and learn to be very quiet and still, God will speak to us. Some call it "the inner voice." I've also come to appreciate how God even speaks through our mouths and through the mouths of those around us. It's no wonder the ancient people called Him "the Great Mysterious One."

My story begins on a very dreary November afternoon in 1985, when, as I recall, things just didn't feel right. It was a Saturday, and my folks had spent the day as usual— shopping and running errands. When I stopped by their house for a minute, my Papa couldn't wait to show me the new shoes he'd bought for all four grandkids he adored.

That's the last time I saw him alive. Within a few hours, my healthy, robust Papa was dead. Never had I experienced such a broken heart or known such weeping.

My Papa's death was just the beginning of many painful endings that intensified my fear of leaving or being left by those I love—which I called life's "comings and goings." Over the next ten years, there would be five other deaths in my immediate family, as well as the pain of caring for several close friends as they were dying.

Through these and other unwelcome transitions in my life, including a divorce, I've learned a lot about what it's like being separated from those you love. I've learned how to ride out the emotional waves and how to find comfort. I've learned more about letting go of the cherished dreams you can lose in a heartbeat. And, most importantly, I've learned that endings are really new beginnings in disguise.

As spiritual beings, we continually die to our old ways to be reborn into a new life. As this process continues, life becomes deeper, richer, and fuller—if we grow in God and in love.

Christ's love is always stronger than the evil in the world, so we need to love and be loved: it's as simple as that.

We can do no great things, only small things with great love.

Each of us has a mission to fulfill: a mission of love. At the hour of death, when we come face-to-face with God, we are going to be judged on love; not on how much we have done, but on how much love we have put into our actions.

Even the rich are hungry for love, for being cared for, for being wanted, for having someone to call their own.

From the abundance of the heart, the mouth speaks. If your heart is full of love, you will speak of love.

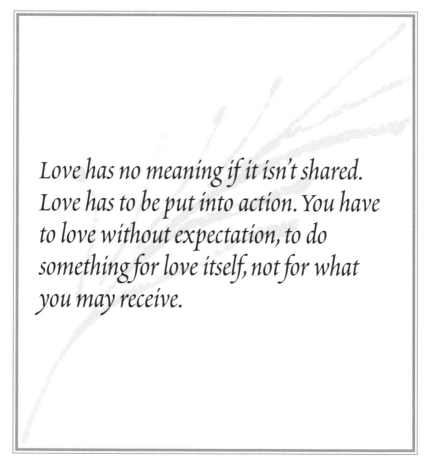

Love has no meaning if it isn't shared. Love has to be put into action. You have to love without expectation, to do something for love itself, not for what you may receive.

In the developed countries, there is a poverty of intimacy, a poverty of spirit, of loneliness, of lack of love. There is no greater sickness in the world today than that one.

I think God is telling us something with AIDS, giving us an opportunity to show our love. People with AIDS have awakened the tender love in those who had perhaps shut it out and forgotten it.

It is not how much you do but how much love you put into the doing and sharing with others that is important.

Faith to be true has to be a giving love. Love and faith go together. They complete each other.

Try not to judge people. If you judge others then you are not giving love. Instead, try to help them by seeing their needs and acting to meet them.

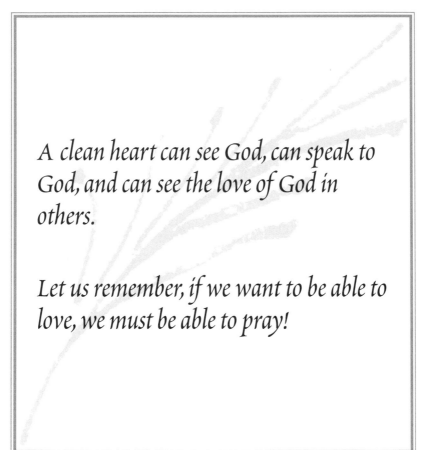

A clean heart can see God, can speak to God, and can see the love of God in others.

Let us remember, if we want to be able to love, we must be able to pray!

Faithfulness to the little things will help us grow in love.

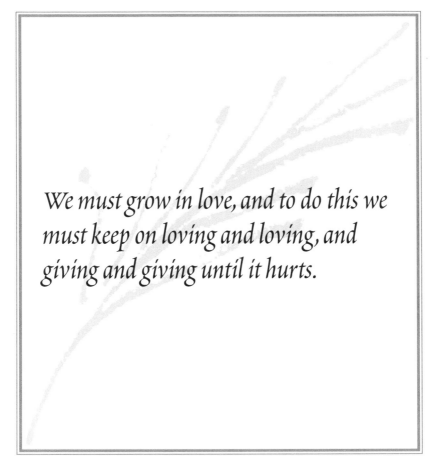

We must grow in love, and to do this we must keep on loving and loving, and giving and giving until it hurts.

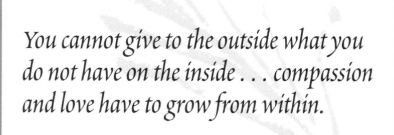

You cannot give to the outside what you do not have on the inside . . . compassion and love have to grow from within.

*Love in action is
what gives us grace.*

We can cure physical diseases with medicine, but the only cure for loneliness, despair, and hopelessness is love.

There are many in the world who are dying for a piece of bread, but there are many more dying for a little love.

"God has not called me to be successful. He called me to be faithful."

—Mother Teresa

II

LETTING GO AND LETTING GOD

Another profound ending came into my life in the fall of 1995. After much soul-searching, I let go of a long, well-established career—a career that for many years had been very gratifying and fulfilling. It meant, of course, that I'd have to leave the people I'd come to love—my work family. But I yearned for something more, and I knew I wanted to grow in new ways.

As a manager in a tough business that was subject to constant public scrutiny and criticism, I couldn't remember a work week shorter than fifty-five or sixty hours. As a single parent, I would come home every night to even greater responsibilities. Life was passing me by; I wanted to slow it down, simplify it, and enjoy it more fully. I longed for the things of the spirit, the simple pleasures that fill me up: music, cooking, writing, quiet walks, and just having more time to be with those I love. I intended to take at least a year off to "catch my breath." God, I think, had other plans.

It was the holiday season; Mother Teresa's book *A Simple Path* had just hit the bookstores. As soon as I saw an ad for it, I knew that I had to read it. In one passage, Mother Teresa talked about the work that the Missionaries of Charity do with AIDS victims and about the first hospices they started in New York City, San Francisco, and Washington, D.C. *Washington, D.C.!* I couldn't believe it— I'd been to D.C. several times already that month, and I'd be going again that January. In an instant I knew what I was meant to do. I had to find my way to Mother Teresa's hospice—I had to see it for myself.

If you don't believe in God, you can help others by doing works of love, and the fruit of these works are the extra graces that come into your soul.

Do what you do best, but do it for the love of God, not fame or riches, and you will begin helping the whole world.

Every work of love, done with a full heart, always brings people closer to God.

Works of love are always works of peace. Whenever you share love with others, you'll notice the peace that comes to you and to them.

We have all been created for greater things—to love and be loved. Love is love—to love a person without any conditions, without any expectations.

Small things, done in great love, bring joy and peace.

Each moment is all we need, not more.
Be happy now and if you show through
your actions that you love others,
including those who are poorer than
you, you'll give them happiness, too.

Love is a fruit in season at all times, and
within reach of every hand. Anyone
may gather it and no limit is set.

To love, it is necessary to give. To give, it is necessary to be free from selfishness.

The most terrible disease that can ever strike a human being is to have no one near him to be loved. Without a heart full of love, without generous hands, it is impossible to cure a man suffering of loneliness.

You must give what will cost you something . . . then your gift becomes a sacrifice, which will have value before God. Any sacrifice is useful if it is done out of love.

Love is proved by deeds; the more they cost us, the greater the proof of our love.

Do ordinary things with extraordinary love.

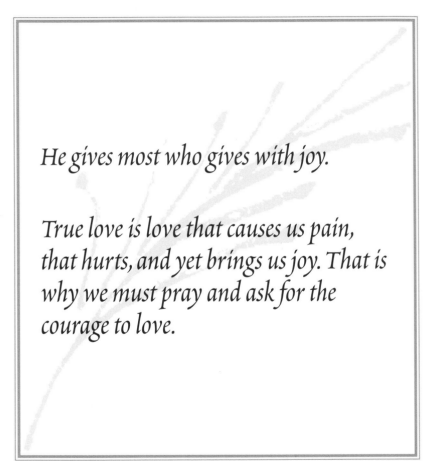

He gives most who gives with joy.

True love is love that causes us pain, that hurts, and yet brings us joy. That is why we must pray and ask for the courage to love.

Prayer begets faith, faith begets love, and love begets service.

"If He wants something to be done,
He will give us the means."

—Mother Teresa

III

THE BLESSING

After arriving in D.C., I wasted no time in calling a number that I had been given for the Missionaries of Charity. I was told, however, that I would have to call back after 9:00 P.M. and that I would need to ask for Sister Pietra.

Later that same night, I followed my instructions carefully, waiting on the line for what seemed like several minutes. Finally, a soft voice said, "Hello, I am Sister Pietra." I began to tell her my story about being a volunteer in an AIDS support group in my community and how my friends and I had helped raise money for a new hospice house where I live. I told her that I had traveled a long way and that I was in D.C. on business. I told her how much I wanted to come and work at their hospice on Saturday.

In a kind way, Sister Pietra said that wasn't possible—that no one is allowed to work there unless they have been

through special training. "When will you be back?" she
asked. "We will be giving another orientation in April." I
explained to Sister Pietra that I really didn't know when
my work would bring me back to D.C., that I was here
now, and I had planned my trip so that I could stay over
that Saturday. Again, she said kindly but firmly, "You
don't understand. I may not even be here this Saturday. It
is impossible."

A bit taken aback, I took a deep breath and began
speaking in words I didn't recognize. "No, Sister. You do
not understand. I need to come because it will bless me. I
need the blessing." And then I began to pour out from my
heart the rest of my story. I told her about my precious
nephew, the one who had always been like my own
child—about his life on the streets and how he had
contracted AIDS by the time he was twenty-two. As Sister
Pietra listened quietly, I told her about how his father, my
only brother, had died when this beloved child was just
two and how estranged my nephew and his mother were
throughout his life. And I told her that, in spite of great
fears, my mother and my sisters and I had brought him
home and cared for him those last weeks he lived because
he longed to be with us. I also shared with her that I had
never known such peace and joy and love, and that in

spite of this being such a sad time in my life, I felt incredibly blessed by it, too.

"So, you see, Sister," I said through my tears, "I need to do this. It will bless me." And, without hesitation, she answered, "Be here at 9:00 A.M. Saturday and ask for me."

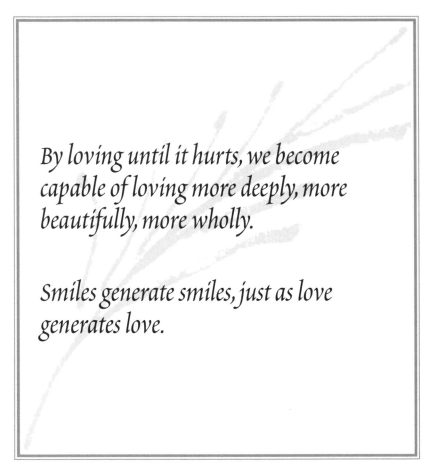

By loving until it hurts, we become capable of loving more deeply, more beautifully, more wholly.

Smiles generate smiles, just as love generates love.

We don't need to look for happiness: If we have love for others, we'll be given it. It is the gift of God.

The world never needed love more than today: people are starving for love.

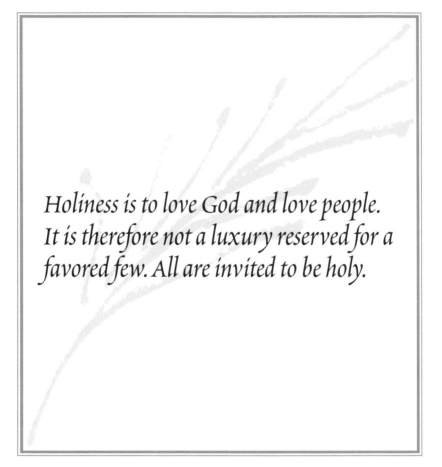

Holiness is to love God and love people.
It is therefore not a luxury reserved for a
favored few. All are invited to be holy.

Love always unites. It does not divide.

You cannot love two people perfectly, but you can love all people perfectly if you love the one Jesus in them all. This means that one should center mind and heart, life, and activity on Jesus, seeing Him in every human sufferer.

Joy is a net of love by which you can catch souls.

We have to pour our love on someone. And people are the means of expressing our love for God.

Let us all keep the joy of loving God in our hearts, and share this joy of loving one another as He loves each one of us.

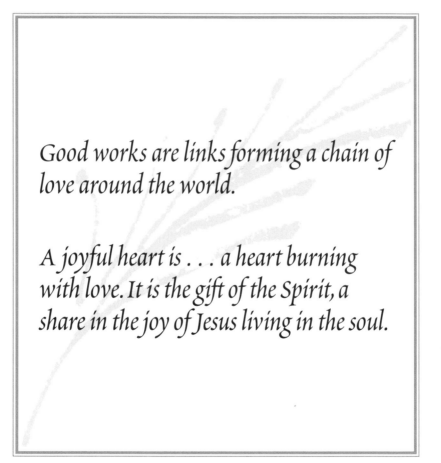

Good works are links forming a chain of love around the world.

A joyful heart is . . . a heart burning with love. It is the gift of the Spirit, a share in the joy of Jesus living in the soul.

What counts is how much love there is in the giving and not how much we give.

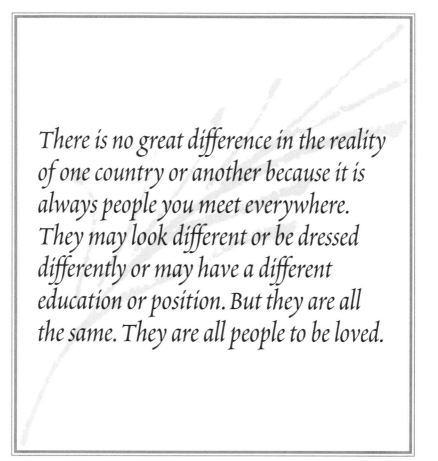

There is no great difference in the reality of one country or another because it is always people you meet everywhere. They may look different or be dressed differently or may have a different education or position. But they are all the same. They are all people to be loved.

Where God is, there is love. And where there is love, there is always service.

"Everybody has something good inside. Some hide it, some neglect it, but it is there."

—Mother Teresa

IV

GIFT OF PEACE

Waiting for a taxi early that Saturday, I remembered the concerns that some colleagues had for my safety. Some doubted whether I'd even be able to get a taxi back downtown once I got out to the hospice. I felt uneasy. The taxi driver made matters worse. Not only was he uncertain about the address I gave him, there was no way he would promise to return for me.

As the taxi took me away, I sat quietly in back, wondering what was next. When we had driven for some time, the taxi driver began to ask me questions about "this place, Gift of Peace." I tried my best to explain about Mother Teresa and the Missionaries of Charity, about their work among the poor and dying around the world—and even here in D.C. He continued to ask me questions, and with each one, I could hear his voice soften. By the time we arrived at the hospice, he turned to me and said, "You go to the door, and I'll wait to make sure someone answers."

When the door opened, I went back to the taxi to pay my fare. Then, in a caring voice, he said, "I really can't promise you anything, but if there's any way that I can be back here at noon to pick you up, I will."

In a fifteen-minute taxi ride, somewhere through the outlying neighborhoods of Washington, D.C.—far from the security of my hotel—I had witnessed a transformation. God, whose love and power is infinite and absolute, had worked in His wonderfully mysterious way. Before my very eyes, He softened the heart of this stranger I had hired to take me safely to Mother Teresa's "Gift of Peace," her spartan hospice on N.E. Otis Street.

Love is giving the best we have.

*Love starts at home and lasts at home
. . . the home is each person's first field of
loving, devotion, and service.*

*It is easy to love people far away. It is
easier to give a cup of rice than to relieve
the loneliness and pain of someone
unloved in our own home.*

We all should become carriers of God's love. But to do this, we must deepen our life of love and prayer and sacrifice.

When you know how much God is in love with you, then you can only live your life radiating that love.

Love begins in the family. Peace begins in the family. Where there is love, there is unity, peace, and joy.

Your suffering is a great means of love, if you make use of it, especially if you offer it for peace in the world.

*I think the world today is upside down.
It is suffering so much because there is so
little love in the home and in family life.
We have no time for our children. We
have no time for each other.*

Love has no other message but its own.

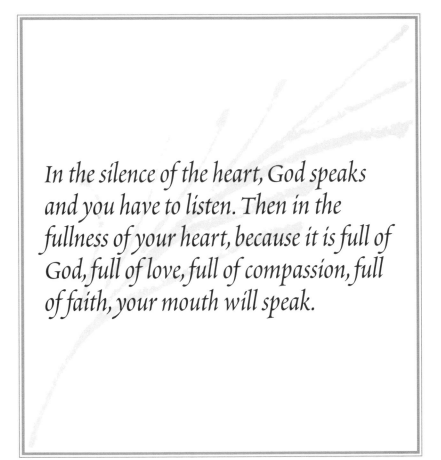

In the silence of the heart, God speaks and you have to listen. Then in the fullness of your heart, because it is full of God, full of love, full of compassion, full of faith, your mouth will speak.

We have all been created in the image of God to love and to be loved.

"Pain, sorrow, feelings of loneliness
are nothing but the kiss of Jesus, a sign that you
have come so close that He can kiss you."

—Mother Teresa

V

IN THE PRESENCE
OF ANGELS

Once I was inside the hospice, any doubt that I had
experienced vanished quickly. I was awed by two things:
the stark simplicity of the hospice and the radiance of the
sisters, clad in their flowing white saris. The contentment
and peace on their faces was undeniable. I knew that I was
in the presence of angels, for sure—these loving sisters
bound, with Mother Teresa, to God in serving others.

When Sister Pietra came to greet me, she quickly took
me to one of the other sisters for my work assignment.
Although I had longed to care for AIDS patients, I was
assigned to help with the morning baths and grooming of
the elderly. For the next three hours, the sisters bathed
individuals, partially dressed them, and then brought them
to me, one-by-one, to powder them, to comb their hair, to

clip their nails—to simply care for them, to be loving with them. Time passed quickly.

Soon, Sister Pietra reappeared. After thanking me for helping out, she pointed down the long basement hallway to a set of doors. "That is the way," she said. As I approached the doors, a sign posted on one caught my attention. It was a scripture from Psalms: "The Lord shall watch over your going out and your coming in from this time forth, forevermore." Without a voice, in the quiet of that dark hallway, God had surely spoken to me and I heard it.

Here I was, almost forty-eight years old—on the outside a woman others had described as strong-willed, decisive, capable. For as long as I could remember, I had been fiercely independent and quite proud of it. But on the inside was this sorrowful little girl who couldn't bear the thought of being separated from one more person she loved—all of the "comings and goings" of life had been far more painful than she could admit, even to herself.

Our life of contemplation, simply put, is to realize God's constant presence and His tender love for us in the least little things of life.

If we pray, our hearts become clean, and we are filled with the love of God—a love that gives without counting the cost; love that is tender and compassionate; love that forgives.

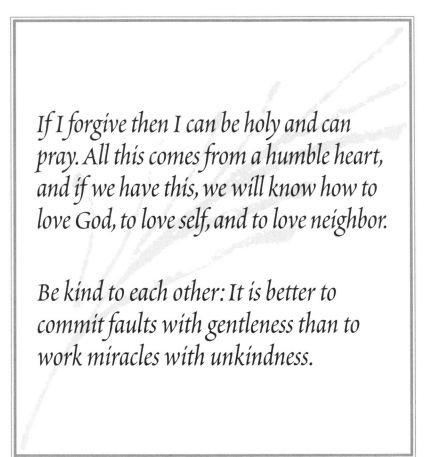

If I forgive then I can be holy and can pray. All this comes from a humble heart, and if we have this, we will know how to love God, to love self, and to love neighbor.

Be kind to each other: It is better to commit faults with gentleness than to work miracles with unkindness.

God loves us with a tender love. That is all that Jesus came to teach us: the tender love of God.

Pray lovingly like children, with an earnest desire to love much and to make loved the one that is not loved.

Loving must be as normal to us as living and breathing, day after day, until our death.

When you feel lonely, when you feel unwanted, when you feel sick and forgotten, remember you are precious to God. He loves you. Show that love for one another.

It is a wonderful thing that God Himself loves me tenderly. That is why we should have courage, joy, and the conviction that nothing can separate us from the love of Christ.

It is the intensity of love we put into our gestures that makes them into something beautiful for God.

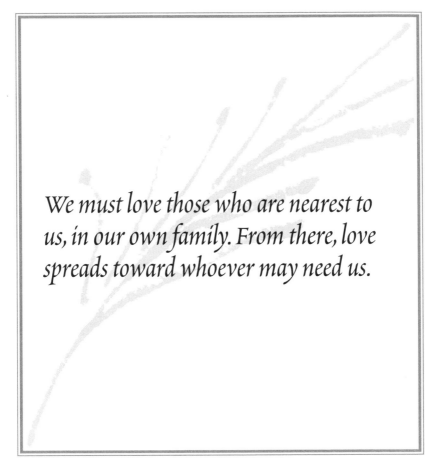

We must love those who are nearest to us, in our own family. From there, love spreads toward whoever may need us.

The fruit of faith is love.

I want you to go and find the poor in your own homes. Above all, your love has to start there.

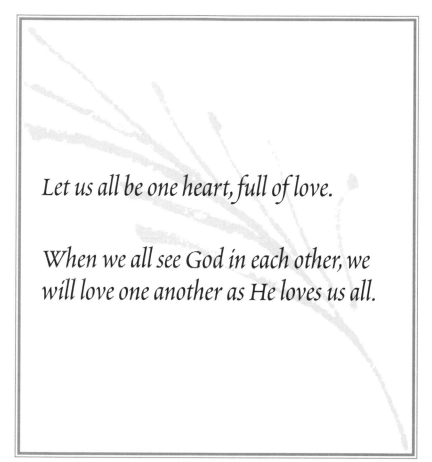

Let us all be one heart, full of love.

When we all see God in each other, we will love one another as He loves us all.

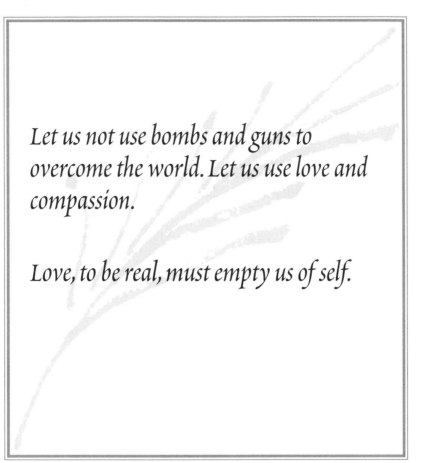

Let us not use bombs and guns to overcome the world. Let us use love and compassion.

Love, to be real, must empty us of self.

There are Danish children who make sacrifices in order to be able to offer others a glass of milk every day. And German children do the same . . . these are concrete ways of teaching love. When these children grow up, they will know what it means to give.

"The meaning of my life is the love of God."

—Mother Teresa

VI

AN ENDLESS LOVE

Why did God lead me to that hospice, far away in Washington, D.C.? And why to Mother Teresa?

Perhaps it's because I longed for constancy. Clearly, Mother Teresa lived with more constancy than most of us. She lived in love—from a heart fully aware that she was doing exactly what God intended for her to do. When we live as she did—perfectly centered in our purpose and using the special gifts that God gives each of us to love and serve others—we are given "the gift of peace." And, God fills us with His love. In a world where nothing seems to last, where there are always "comings and goings" and much uncertainty, we are never really alone. God is always in us. We are never separated from Him or His love.

To this day I'm still growing in my understanding of that experience on N.E. Otis Street. Without realizing it, I'd been on a spiritual journey for a very long time. Every death and separation had been a painful part of that journey. I'd been dying to the old "realities" only to be reborn into a deeper, richer, fuller understanding of myself and of the God who lives in me, who is with me always and whose love is endless. I'd been learning to live in love.

That is my wish for you. May you also know that the Great Mysterious One—whose love and power triumphs over all things, is absolute and never ending—watches over your "going out and your coming in," too.

Give of your hands to serve and your hearts to love.

What matters is the gift of yourself, the degree of love you put into each one of your actions.

Let us not be satisfied with just paying money. Money is not enough. Money can be got. The poor need your hands to serve them. They need your heart to love them.

In order for us to be able to love, we need to have faith because faith is love in action, and love in action is service.

Be an angel of comfort to the sick, a friend to the little ones, and love each other as God loves each one of you with a special, most intense love.

Love, an abundant love, is the expression of our Christian religion.

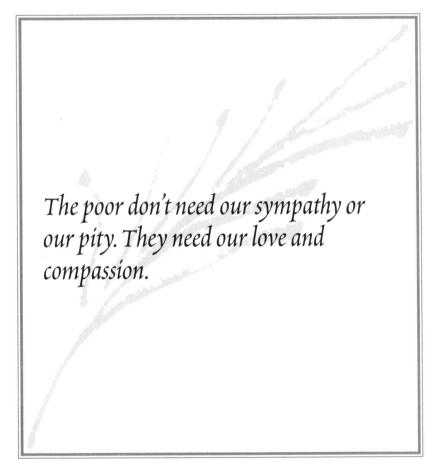

The poor don't need our sympathy or our pity. They need our love and compassion.

It is a gift of God to be able to share our love with others.

Our lives, to be beautiful, must be full of thought for others.

To love with a pure heart, to love everybody, especially to love the poor, is a twenty-four-hour prayer.

Each one of us must be able to say: I will be love.

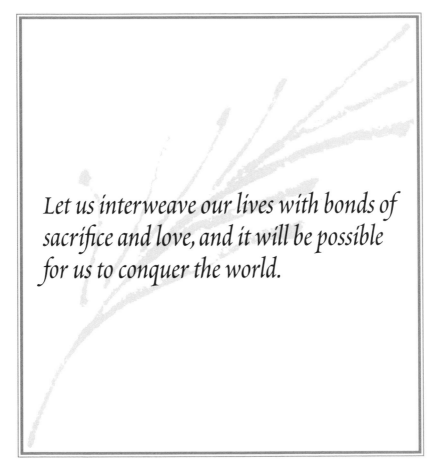

Let us interweave our lives with bonds of sacrifice and love, and it will be possible for us to conquer the world.

The world is lost for want of sweetness and kindness.

Those of you who are sick, when things are hard, take refuge in Christ's heart. There, my own heart will find you with strength and love.

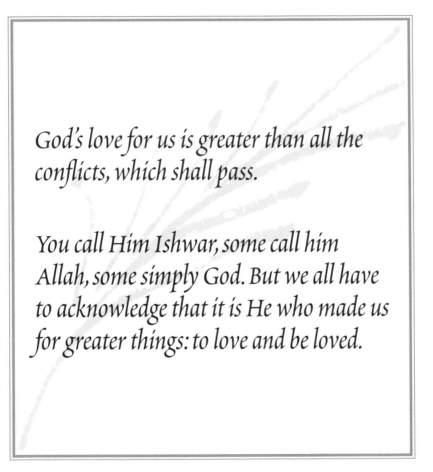

God's love for us is greater than all the conflicts, which shall pass.

You call Him Ishwar, some call him Allah, some simply God. But we all have to acknowledge that it is He who made us for greater things: to love and be loved.

Every child is a sign of God's love.

BIBLIOGRAPHY

Bartos, Pat. "Someone Beautiful Goes to God." *Our Sunday Visitor,* September 21, 1997 (Vol. 86, No. 21), pp. 2–23.

Beneate, Becky and Joseph Duprepos, editors. *No Greater Love.* Novato, Calif.: New World Library, 1997, pp. 4, 9, 13–16, 20–24, 26–30, 32, 38, 42, 58, 98, 125, 128–129, 136, 137, 179.

Beneate, Becky, editor. *In the Heart of the World.* Novato, Calif.: New World Library, 1997, pp. 13, 29, 40, 42, 45, 60, 107.

Commemorative Program, Père Marquette Discovery Award, presented to Mother Teresa at Marquette University, June 1981.

Doig, Desmond. *Mother Teresa, Her People and Her Work.* New York: Harper & Row, 1976, p. 162.

Egan, Eileen. *Such a Vision of the Street: Mother Teresa, the Spirit and the Work.* Garden City, N.Y.: Doubleday, 1985, pp. 220, 324, 341, 357.

Gonzalez-Balado, Jose Luis, and Janet N. Playfoot, editors. *My Life for the Poor: Mother Teresa of Calcutta.* San Francisco: Harper & Row, 1985, pp. 33, 37, 44, 57, 72, 73, 100, 104.

LaPierre, Dominique. *Compassion; Mother Teresa Persists with Love.* New York Times News Service, December 25, 1994.

LeJoly, Edward. *Mother Teresa of Calcutta: A Biography.* San Francisco: Harper & Row, 1985, pp. 161, 177, 179, 180, 185, 211, 255.

Mother Teresa, "Letter to Friends of the Missionaries of Charity," March 12, 1996.

Muggeridge, Malcolm. *Something Beautiful for God; Mother Teresa of Calcutta.* New York: Harper & Row, 1971, pp. 65, 72, 73, 98, 112.

Prince Michael of Greece. "All the Lives We Touch," *Parade,* August 11, 1996, pp. 4–5.

Rai, Raghu, and Navin Chawala, *The Life and Work of Mother Teresa.* Rockport, Mass.: Element Books, 1996, pp. 90, 158, 191, 192.

Shelton, Karen Eberhardt. "The Woman Who Loved the World," *Family Circle,* February 17, 1998, p. 154.

Vardey, Lucinda, compiler, *Mother Teresa: A Simple Path,* New York: Ballantine Books, 1995, pp. 7–8, 40, 43, 52, 80–81, 87, 93, 99, 101, 108, 171, 181.

THE AUTHOR

Glenna Hammer Moulthrop, a former communications executive with Westinghouse, owns a consulting business in government and public affairs and fundraising. During a twenty-five-year career in communications and newspaper reporting, Moulthrop won dozens of writing and editing awards. However, it was her very first award—earned as a third-grader— for a review of "The Story of Jesus" that still means the most to her. As an eight-year-old reviewing the book, she simply wrote, "It made me feel good inside."

Moulthrop lives with her two college-age daughters in the Tri-Cities of Washington, where she also serves on the board of several community organizations. It is the Tri-Cities Chaplaincy Hospice House and Counseling Center, however, that has her heart. She organizes the center's two largest fundraisers each year and assists in many programs that help the troubled, the dying, and those struggling with HIV/AIDS.

A portion of the royalties from this book
will be donated to the Missionaries of Charity
in loving memory of Mother Teresa
(August 26, 1910–September 5, 1997).